Steve Austin
The Story of the Wrestler They Call "Stone Cold"

Bill Goldberg

Bret Hart
The Story of the Wrestler They Call "The Hitman"

The Story of the Wrestler
They Call "Hollywood" Hulk Hogan

Randy Savage
The Story of the Wrestler They Call "Macho Man"

The Story of the Wrestler They Call "Sting"

The Story of the Wrestler They Call "The Undertaker"

Jesse Ventura
The Story of the Wrestler They Call "The Body"

CHELSEA HOUSE PUBLISHERS

Bill Goldberg

Kyle Alexander

Chelsea House Publishers
Philadelphia

Produced by Choptank Syndicate, Inc.

Editor and Picture Researcher: Mary Hull
Design and Production: Lisa Hochstein

CHELSEA HOUSE PUBLISHERS

Editor in Chief: Stephen Reginald
Managing Editor: James D. Gallagher
Production Manager: Pamela Loos
Art Director: Sara Davis
Director of Photography: Judy L. Hasday
Senior Production Editor: LeeAnne Gelletly
Cover Illustrator: Keith Trego

Cover Photos: WCW
              Sports Action

The Chelsea House World Wide Web site
address is http://www.chelseahouse.com

First Printing

1 3 5 7 9 8 6 4 2

Library of Congress Cataloging-in-Publication Data

Alexander, Kyle
    Bill Goldberg / Kyle Alexander
       p. cm.—(Pro wrestling legends)
    Includes bibliographical references (p.) and index.
    Summary: A biography of the professional football player turned
wrestler who made his World Championship Wrestling debut in 1997
and won more than 170 matches as a rookie.
    ISBN   0-7910-5404-7 (hc) — 0-7910-5550-7 (pb)
    1. Goldberg, Bill, 1966– Juvenile literature. 2. Wrestlers—United States—
Biography—Juvenile literature. [1. Goldberg, Bill, 1966– . 2. Wrestlers.]
I. Title. II. Series.
GV1196.G65A44 1999
796.8'12'092—dc21
[B]   99-32899
                                                      CIP

Contents

CHAPTER 1
WHO'S NEXT?   7

CHAPTER 2
TRANSITIONS   15

CHAPTER 3
THE STREAK   23

CHAPTER 4
THE CHAMPION   33

CHAPTER 5
THE SHOCKING LOSS   41

CHAPTER 6
NEW CHALLENGES   51

Chronology   61

Further Reading   62

Index   63

WHO'S NEXT?

There was a new face in the locker-room area of World Championship Wrestling (WCW) on the evening of September 22, 1997. An unknown wrestler was about to make his professional debut in front of millions of wrestling fans tuning in to the popular WCW *Monday Nitro* broadcast. As the man prepared for his moment in the spotlight, few of the other wrestlers paid much attention to him. At 6' 4" and 285 pounds of pure muscle, the newcomer was hard not to notice; still, there are a lot of dues one must pay before the athletes of the sport will pay anyone any real measure of respect. That's just how the wrestling business works.

Suddenly, a scream and a loud, crashing sound filled the quiet locker room, startling all its occupants.

As was his custom in preparing for a game in his previous sport of football, the rookie slammed his head into a nearby locker. The sickening sound of skull hitting metal stunned everyone in the room, who watched in wonder as the power-house left the room and headed toward the ring.

For this athlete, it was just another personal tradition, his way of getting into what he calls "the zone."

He quietly waited behind the curtain for his name to be called, still focused on his task. This was uncharted territory

---

Bill Goldberg made his World Championship Wrestling debut on September 22, 1997, when he was paired against Hugh Morrus during a live Monday Nitro *broadcast.*

for a man who, for most of his life, had competed on the gridiron as a football star. No teammates to his left or right to protect his play. No pads on his arms or legs to protect his bones. No helmet to protect his skull, still pounding from the impact with the locker.

Unfamiliarity surrounded him as he faced an arena full of fans who had no idea who he was. Fans traditionally overlook the preliminary wrestlers. The stereotype portrays them as inexperienced athletes who never win matches. They just end up making their opponents look good.

This newcomer was intent on making nobody look good . . . except himself.

He walked slowly to the ring. Along the way, he caught a glance here and there from an audience that did not seem all that impressed. He overheard fans making comments such as, "Who is this guy?" and, "Oh, great, another muscle man." He was safe in assuming that most fans in the arena did not come there that night to see him wrestle. His goal was to make them notice him.

But first, he would have to make his opponent notice him.

Hugh Morrus, his professional foe on that evening, may have felt the same way about his adversary as the fans did. "Just another day at the office," he must have thought to himself.

Who would have thought that everyone in the arena that night, including Morrus, could have been so wrong?

At 5' 10" and 230 pounds, Morrus is not the largest competitor in WCW, but he has won his share of matches. When he was slated to face an unknown wrestler on this live *Nitro* broadcast, he shrugged it off as another easy match.

He was simply looking to improve his record and move another rung up the ladder of contention toward the WCW World title.

There were two things standing in Morrus's way on that fateful September evening. The first was destiny. The second was the man standing across from him, Bill Goldberg.

WCW did not air any promotional videos on Goldberg leading up to the match. There was no press conference to announce that he had signed with WCW. Those are attention-getting devices reserved for established stars who enter the promotion. Frankly, there just was not much interest in him at the time. He was just one man, unknown to wrestling fans, walking to the ring to face the more experienced Morrus.

Even the television announcers that evening had little information on Goldberg. They knew that he was a former football player who had just graduated from WCW's training camp known as the "Power Plant," and that he was making a difficult transition from professional football to professional wrestling. As the match prepared to get under way, their commentary focused on other matches scheduled for later that evening and on a future pay-per-view event.

The two men faced each other in the ring. Morrus lived up to his nickname of the "Laughing Man" by giggling as he looked into the steely eyes of his foe. Goldberg was not amused. His cleanly shaved head bobbed and twitched, but he remained silent and intent. No words. No "trash talking." The silence that he showed in the ring would be a silence that defined the first few months of his career.

Goldberg's wrestling attire was simple and basic: black trunks and matching boots. Many

Bill Goldberg was a defensive tackle for the Atlanta Falcons from 1992 to 1994. While living in Atlanta, the home of WCW, he had the opportunity to meet and socialize with pro wrestlers like Sting, Lex Luger, and "Diamond" Dallas Page.

fans in attendance were comparing his look to that of the World Wrestling Federation (WWF) superstar "Stone Cold" Steve Austin. Some even left their seats to get a refreshment or take a break from the action.

What they and Morrus did not know—but would find out soon—was that this match truly had magnitude.

The bout started slowly as each man attempted to figure out what the other would do next. Without the advantage of video or scouting reports, Morrus had no information on Goldberg. "Not to worry," Morrus must have thought to himself, "I've faced these kinds of guys before. They're a dime a dozen."

Morrus made the critical mistake of engaging in tests of strength with Goldberg; he got nowhere. For the next several minutes, he continued to get nowhere, no matter what type of offense he attempted. What was to be a standard preliminary match for the more experienced Morrus was turning into a bout that was anything but standard.

Morrus grew more anxious and began to lose focus. As any opponent who has faced Goldberg since his debut will attest: when you lose your focus and confidence, you have lost the match. Goldberg smells that like a shark smells blood.

The announcers began to take notice of what was happening in the ring. They put aside their pay-per-view notes and started scrambling for something to say about this unknown commodity who was looking like he might give Morrus a competitive match, if not win it outright. Fans were noticing it too.

Before anyone could take much time to think about what was happening, Goldberg gave them something to really notice. He took Morrus and lifted him in the air, as if to suplex him (a move in which a wrestler places his opponent in a headlock, lifts him in the air, and flips him over his back). Instead Goldberg shifted his body weight to land on the Laughing Man as they crashed onto the mat.

The move had a name. Goldberg called it the "jackhammer." Later on, he would offer an explanation: "It's basically holding a guy upside-down straight in the air, and, when the time is right, I drop him right on his back and he doesn't get up from that."

Indeed. On that September night, the devastation of the move sent pain throughout Morrus's massive frame. The referee delivered the three-count. Shock rippled through the arena. Hugh Morrus, along with everyone else watching, was introduced to the jackhammer, and to Bill Goldberg, who had just won his pro debut.

It was the first step in an unprecedented undefeated streak.

The fans were stunned. The announcers were speechless. Morrus still could not move. Here was a wrestler fresh out of training overpowering and pinning an experienced and established WCW star.

Initially, some said that Morrus had underestimated his stronger opponent. Others said that Goldberg simply got lucky and proved the timeless wrestling adage that any given man can be beaten by any opponent on any given night. Goldberg's victory was seen as something of a fluke. As the wrestlers watched the match on monitors in the dressing room, it was generally agreed that Morrus was off his game, and that Goldberg could easily be handled. If anything, they reasoned, a rookie is predictable in his first few matches.

Before long, the prediction for a Goldberg match would become strikingly clear: decisive victory—for Goldberg.

After the upset win over Morrus, Goldberg walked back to the locker room. There were no well-wishers waiting for him. There was no victory celebration. Nobody knew quite what to make of this powerful new presence in their midst. Above all, nobody suspected what lay ahead, not the other wrestlers, not the broadcasters, not the fans, and certainly not Goldberg himself.

"I just take things one step at a time," Goldberg would say in a later interview. "Sure, that's a commonly used cliche, but, in my case, it's very true."

Step one had taken place just the way Goldberg wanted: he entered the ring an unknown, and left it a winner. Best of all, there was electricity in the air. The fans knew they had witnessed something special, and they couldn't wait to see more.

For his part, Goldberg couldn't wait to give it to them. Of course, nobody realized at the time that an era was beginning on that evening. They did, however, know that a mid-card newcomer had beaten the odds in a big way.

Goldberg was no stranger to beating the odds.

In contrast to his ring entrances, William Goldberg entered the world without fireworks or fanfare. He was born on December 27, 1966, in Tulsa, Oklahoma, the youngest of Ethel and Jed Goldberg's four children.

He was born into a "football family" in which the gridiron game was as important as any other element of daily life. The pigskin was a familiar item in the household, as familiar as the windows that it occasionally shattered.

Goldberg's older brothers were football stars at Tulsa's Edison High School. Mike was a talented defensive lineman, while Steve divided his time between linebacker and kicker. Both achieved All-State honors and were highly recruited by major colleges around the country. The Goldberg brothers would end up at the University of Minnesota.

His brothers' influence weighed heavily on the life of young William. Images of Mike and Steve dominating on the field were constantly on display for the wide-eyed child. The powerful tackles, devastating body blows, and overall intensity of the competition thrilled and inspired the impressionable boy.

The family tradition would definitely continue.

William officially started his football competition in the eighth grade and, from the start, his goal was simple: seek

---

When he first surfaced in the WCW, the only thing announcers knew about Bill Goldberg was that he had been a pro football player (number 71) and was now trying to make it in pro wrestling.

and destroy. A tackle was not merely knocking another player to the ground. He wanted to take that rival violently to the ground and send a clear message: getting up from a Goldberg tackle would be difficult, if not impossible.

At the tender age of 15, he was already gaining a reputation as someone to be feared.

"He had that snarl and love of the game," said Jim Cherry, football coach at Edison High, "and he was born for football. He was 6' 3", 250 pounds with a full beard when I first saw him as a ninth-grader."

Cherry was not the only one who noticed William's intensity and fierce dedication. Colleges soon came calling for Goldberg's services, and scouts marveled at his willingness to put his body on the line for a victory.

Goldberg's parents had instilled strong morals and ethics in all their children. In William's case, those lessons included the imperatives to be unique and set goals above his own expectations. On the way to achieving those goals, he was taught to treat others the way he would want to be treated.

Most of all, William was told to stay within the rules. He could grunt and growl to his heart's content. He could powerfully careen his body into a member of the opposing team. Beneath it all, though, fair play always had to be the foundation of all that he did.

William echoed his brothers' success on the high school football field. He received All-City and All-State honors, including Defensive Player of the Year. His senior year was the pinnacle of his high school career. The dream of elevating his football career to the next level was about to be realized.

Then William's dream was interrupted by the first of many stunning life setbacks.

His parents decided to separate and divorce. Suddenly, his solid support system was in disarray. His brothers were off living lives of their own, and the high school senior felt as if he were left to fend for himself. Forget his opponents; his self-esteem had been tackled to the ground. He felt responsible for his mother and father's divorce.

Somehow, William found a way to overcome the guilt and move on to a new, and somewhat uncertain, chapter in his life.

He decided that the University of Georgia would be his next field of battle, so he left the safety and security of his Tulsa home behind. For the first time in his life, he would have to fend for himself. For the first time in his life, he would not be surrounded by family and friends. But one thing remained the same: Goldberg's desire to get back on the football field.

Becoming a member of the Georgia Bulldogs football team, he felt, would be perfect. He would join the legendary "Dawg Pound." Intimidation became his trademark. He walked with a confident swagger. He barked, growled, and snarled just as he did in high school, but with a college-level intensity.

Self-discipline and a strong sense of responsibility pushed Goldberg to excel on the gridiron. Among the wide variety of awards and recognition he received, he became a two-time All-SEC defender with 348 tackles to his credit—seventh best in the school's history.

Vince Dooley, his coach, also saw the raw potential and killer instinct of his young student. He provided key guidance to Goldberg both on

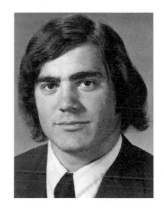

The youngest child in a family that loved football, Bill Goldberg grew up playing the game with his older brothers Mike (top) and Steve (bottom), who earned All-State honors and were recruited by the University of Minnesota.

and off the field. Dooley was a mentor to a man who was still seeking guidance from those he respected and revered.

"He was always a great competitor," said Dooley, now the University's athletic director. "He's a relentless athlete that would hit you so hard your teeth would shake."

Four years were a blur for Goldberg, as he earned not only legendary status on the gridiron, but also a degree in psychology. The challenges at Georgia were over, and it was time for him to face a new hurdle, the National Football League (NFL). He was ranked among the top 52 players in the nation. A draft into a pro team was inevitable.

Another dream was about to come true. But another setback was also about to occur.

Before the draft, Goldberg became ill. His weight dropped, and he was unable to compete in an important practice held in full view of NFL coaches. He ended up being drafted later than predicted by the Los Angeles Rams.

Goldberg was determined to turn this negative into a positive, despite the fact that his reputation had decreased significantly. His goal now was to overwhelm the Rams's coaches with the skills and attitude that he had developed in both high school and college. The "bark" was still in that "Dawg," but adversity would once again get in his way in the form of an injury before the season started.

The Rams cut him from their roster.

Even this monumental setback would not discourage Goldberg. The guidance of his parents, siblings, and a beloved coach remained with him and provided him with the motivation he needed. Goldberg simply had to play football.

It was his identity. He decided to continue his football career with the World Football League.

After competing with the Sacramento Surge, momentum was now on Goldberg's side as the Atlanta Falcons took notice of the aggressive competitor. He was invited to their training camp, and eventually signed with the team.

His dream of playing in the NFL was finally coming true.

Goldberg played with great enthusiasm and intensity. Barking, biting, and snarling, his teammates and coaches loved his fire as much as his opponents feared it. The road to the NFL was so tough for Goldberg, he never wanted to take it for granted. Every day, every game, and every tackle had to have impact.

Being in the NFL spotlight allowed Goldberg to socialize with other famous athletes as well. The headquarters of WCW was based in Atlanta, and the wrestlers and football players often spent time with each other. Men like "Diamond" Dallas Page, Lex Luger, and Sting called Goldberg their friend.

The 1994 season brought continued success, but during that campaign, Goldberg suffered a career-threatening injury: an abdominal tear. Knowing that inactivity could lead to another setback, Goldberg played with pain for the remainder of the season.

During the off-season, Goldberg had surgery to repair the tear and was hopeful about returning to the Falcons the following year. The Falcons, however, viewed the injury as too serious to take a chance on Goldberg coming back, no matter what fire and spirit he displayed. While appreciative of his efforts and dedication, they left him open for an expansion draft.

As a senior at the University of Georgia, number 95 Bill Goldberg led the Bulldogs squad with 121 tackles—a single season record for a lineman— and his 348 career stops were the seventh best in the university's history.

Goldberg found a new home with the Carolina Panthers . . . but not for long.

The injury was not healing. Goldberg knew that he would probably never be able to play football at 100-percent strength ever again. According to his standards, it was an unacceptable situation. So on his own terms, Goldberg quietly retired and ended a football career that had started with a football in his cradle.

For Goldberg, the dream of a lifetime was over.

Now what? Without football, what would his goals be? He could be a trainer, but that would never satisfy his desire to compete.

As he reflected on his past and planned for his future, Goldberg recalled his association with the wrestlers of WCW. As a child, he had casually followed wrestling, but had not considered himself a rabid fan in a household oriented around football.

"Here and there, on Saturdays, I saw wrestling matches on the TV," said Goldberg. "But they weren't as interesting for me as football. I dreamed of playing football." For Goldberg, life had been unpredictable and unfair. A dream had turned to ashes; now a new dream had to be fashioned out of those ashes.

"I was injured, and I had to think about the future," Goldberg recalled. "Lex Luger and Sting, I knew them for many years already, and practiced in their gym, and they've always told me I should wrestle. Until my injury, I didn't think about it seriously."

Goldberg joined WCW officially in September of 1996 and underwent intensive training at WCW's camp, The Power Plant, under the direction of Dwayne Bruce. Along with the friends Goldberg had made from his football days, Arn Anderson also had a hand in his development as a wrestler. They all saw the raw talent in Goldberg, who was starting to enjoy his newfound profession.

He was showing everyone who would notice that he had the killer instinct necessary to compete in the squared circle.

3 THE STREAK

Goldberg found a new life for himself, a life where individual accomplishments stood out over anything else. One year after putting his signature on a WCW contract, Goldberg was ready to unleash the fury that had intimidated football players for so many years. Wrestlers would now feel the impact that Goldberg had made on the field. They would hear the snarl and feel the bite.

Goldberg's motto is "Force equals mass times acceleration." At 6' 4" and 285 pounds, Goldberg has the mass and acceleration to make sure his motto is more forceful than just talk. Defeating a veteran like Hugh Morrus in his first match was an accomplishment that Goldberg could have carried around with him forever.

But Goldberg is not a man who looks back on his achievements. He's always looking forward.

One week after his stunning victory, Goldberg was scheduled to face the Barbarian. While the Barbarian's accomplishments had been primarily in tag team wrestling, he was still feared for his devastating power and lightning speed. One of his boots to the face could end a match, if not a wrestler's career. Perhaps the rookie with a record of 1–0 had finally met his match in just his second bout.

Following his debut in the fall of 1997, Goldberg continued to chalk up victory after victory. Critics thought his streak would end when he faced WCW's top stars, but the critics were wrong.

But Goldberg proved again on that night that winning matches for him was anything but a fluke. He defeated the Barbarian in the same manner he defeated Morrus, the manner that would soon become Goldberg's trademark as a wrestler.

Overwhelm, dominate, and defeat.

Fans looked on with amazement at his growing undefeated streak. It wasn't the numbers that made them take note of Goldberg; it was the way he was achieving those numbers. His matches were not even close to being competitive. Each bout resembled a massacre, with Goldberg the overwhelming, overpowering victor.

His parents looked on with amazement as well. Their son's new athletic direction confused them. While they agreed that his football career was indeed over, they wondered if perhaps he should have taken another career route. Trading in a football helmet for wrestling trunks was not quite what they had in mind for their son.

"When I told them I was starting a new career in the ring, they thought I lost it," recalled Goldberg. "But they knew that if I came to a certain conclusion, it was after doubts and considerations. I made clear I don't intend to be 'just' a wrestler." As Goldberg achieved one win after another, his parents started to accept their son's new life. This "football family" was now becoming a "wrestling family." Their skepticism had been replaced with enthusiasm.

"Right now I'm a wrestling fan," Goldberg's mom proudly announced.

Even as a wrestler, Goldberg still heeded the words of his father and mother. He continued to be disciplined and to respect his fellow athletes.

He set his standards high and refused to stop until his goals were reached. Most of all, Goldberg always played fair.

He was not "just a wrestler"; he was becoming a sensation. Veteran wrestlers, confident that they could show this rookie true competition, challenged Goldberg. As Goldberg wrestled more matches, videotapes of those matches were widely circulated. Wrestlers eager to grab some attention for themselves by halting the Goldberg juggernaut searched for weaknesses in Goldberg's style.

Scotty Riggs, Wrath, Glacier, and Stevie Ray all entered the ring with confidence. Each man

Steve McMichael, another pro football player-turned-wrestler, wanted to be the only two-sport star in WCW. McMichael challenged Goldberg four times without a win.

felt he had the key to beat him. Each man left with another loss added to his record.

Another ex-professional football player turned wrestler, Steve McMichael, had an issue to settle with Goldberg as well. "Mongo" felt he had the exclusive claim to being a two-sport star in WCW. McMichael had only a year more experience than Goldberg in the ring, but he was confident that he could hand Goldberg his first defeat.

The final score for McMichael was four matches with four defeats.

With every win, Goldberg was gaining valuable experience. He learned quickly how to counter a variety of opponents and their moves. Big men. Small men. High-flying moves. Scientific mat maneuvers. It did not matter. He used the defensive skills he had gained in football to baffle his opponents, and he soaked up new wrestling knowledge like a sponge. Every bout showed a new side of Goldberg.

He hungrily absorbed what he had learned from his opponents, and before long he began adding new moves to his repertoire. The jackhammer was effective, but he needed more than just one finishing move. He had to use moves that would make an opponent more vulnerable to that devastating finisher. One move, in particular, proved to complement the jackhammer perfectly: "the spear."

The spear was Goldberg's way of incorporating his football past into his wrestling future. Simply stated, the spear is a crippling tackle in which Goldberg horizontally hurtles his powerful physique into his standing opponent. With the air forced from his lungs, the victim folds around Goldberg's massive frame and then collapses to the ground.

Weak and unable to breathe, the dazed wrestler is now prepared for the jackhammer.

Ouch.

Goldberg had done an excellent job of incorporating his football knowledge into his wrestling style. In doing so, he maintained the killer instinct and deadly intensity that had scared so many offensive linemen.

His intensity and independence, however, were sending mixed signals.

Fans and wrestlers were beginning to believe that Goldberg favored rulebreaking. He did not smile. He did not speak. He grunted, growled, and barked. All his "talking" was done in the ring. No one knew what was going on in his mind. All anyone saw was a frighteningly steely stare from a very unemotional face.

"I want to be different from the others. I want to believe it's hard to define me and put me to the category of 'good' or 'bad,'" said Goldberg. "It's me, doing what I know how to do, and everyone can define and classify me as they wish."

Fans did not take kindly to Goldberg. They felt he was cold and disconnected from them. He did not bother acknowledging them, so they began to boo louder with every one of his victories. The more he ignored their scorn, the louder the jeers became.

Rumors even circulated that Goldberg was soon to join the New World Order (NWO). That evil group was always looking for new recruits in their war with WCW. The more powerful and the more fearful, the better. Goldberg seemed to be a perfect match.

Goldberg managed to break free from Sting's headlock and pin the four-time World champion during their match on June 13, 1998. Goldberg's victory over Sting brought the rookie wrestler both respect and admiration.

But when the opportunity came to pick sides, Goldberg, a team player, decided to be his own man and come to the aid of WCW. He wanted nothing to do with "Hollywood" Hogan and his gang of thugs. Fans were pleasantly surprised, and the chants of "Goldberg" started to be heard in the arenas. Now he had an additional weapon in his arsenal: crowd support.

Meanwhile, the undefeated streak continued, and Goldberg edged into the elite Top 10 listing of World championship contenders.

Nearly seven months into his unprecedented, unblemished career, Goldberg received his first opportunity at a title. He was granted a U.S. championship match with the winner of the Raven–"Diamond" Dallas Page match at WCW's Spring Stampede pay-per-view event on April 19, 1998. The championship match would take place a day later at the same setting that had ushered in his storied career: *Monday Nitro.*

Raven, a moody wrestler who favors T-shirts and jeans over wrestling attire, won the Spring Stampede match against Page. He had the edge on Goldberg in experience, and he also had a reputation for throwing fists and using hidden weapons to gain victories. Raven's violent "in-your-face" style could match up to his opponent's very well.

A spear and a jackhammer proved otherwise.

In the same shocking manner that he won his first bout, Goldberg dominated and destroyed Raven, whose U.S. title reign ended after one day. Goldberg's had begun. Some wrestlers never capture a major championship in their career. Others wait years for just a chance. Goldberg captured the gold while still a rookie.

Goldberg had now passed the 100–0 mark in his unbeaten streak. He had won the hearts of the fans as well as a championship belt. But there was one element still missing.

Respect.

While everyone who saw Goldberg wrestle was impressed, there was still an element of doubt surrounding the new champion. Had he assembled his record by beating a lengthy string of mid-card and preliminary wrestlers? Was he ducking the main event stars of WCW in an effort to keep his record perfect?

On June 13, 1998, Goldberg would answer those questions and end those doubts.

WCW was holding an event in Pittsburgh, Pennyslvania. Goldberg was set to face the 7' 4", 500-pound monster called "The Giant." The Giant, whose real name is Paul Wight, had experienced his own share of rookie success when he won the WCW World title in his first pro year. Many people considered The Giant's talent comparable to that of WWF wrestling legend Andre the Giant. There was no doubt that The Giant was an intimidating challenger who created fear in the hearts of all his opponents.

This would be the most difficult challenge of Goldberg's young career.

Transportation problems forced The Giant to miss the important confrontation. An opponent needed to be found quickly. One man stepped forward to attempt to do what no one had done up to that time: defeat Goldberg.

That man was Sting.

Sting is a genuine WCW superstar—a four-time World champion. Sting had strength, agility, and, most of all, experience.

Fans did not choose sides in this bout. They showed respect for both men as they faced each other in the ring. Again, Goldberg was poker-faced as he stared at Sting's painted face. The "Stinger" was able to counter Goldberg's power for several minutes, but he soon discovered what other opponents had learned in their matches with the U.S. champ.

With a spear and a jackhammer, Goldberg gained a decisive victory over a WCW living legend.

Pinning Sting did something that more than 100 victories and a U.S. title could not. The win gave Goldberg the respect and legitimacy he desired. His own critics now recognized him as a dedicated and still-developing wrestler who had faced the greatest challenge of his career and emerged victorious.

Greater challenges awaited, and new questions began to be asked. Could he win it all? Could he win the WCW World heavyweight title?

Could he defeat "Hollywood" Hulk Hogan?

4 THE CHAMPION

As Goldberg's unbeaten streak grew with every spear and jackhammer, the question "Who's next?" became his motto. What man could possibly stop him? Where would the streak end? Most important, where would this streak take him?

The answer to the last question would be the WCW World heavyweight title.

The man in charge of WCW's executive committee, James J. Dillon, made the announcement on June 30, 1998. In recognition of Goldberg's impressive record, the committee deemed him the number one contender for the World title held by "Hollywood" Hulk Hogan.

The match would take place the following week on the nationally televised live broadcast of WCW *Monday Nitro*.

The Georgia Dome in Atlanta was sold out on the night of July 6. Many fans sensed that history was about to be made. Goldberg had incredible momentum on his side; his record had swelled to 106–0. He had the U.S. heavyweight title belt around his waist. The man who had held such high standards for himself would not settle for second best.

He wanted more. He wanted Hogan.

Winning the WCW U.S. title just seven months after his debut made Bill Goldberg the number one contender for the World title held by "Hollywood" Hulk Hogan.

As *Nitro* went on the air, Hogan couldn't wait to give his official response to the committee that had forced this match upon him. With his NWO cohorts beside him, he walked to the ring and addressed the hostile crowd.

Boos and garbage rained down on the champion as he took the microphone to say what was on his mind.

"This match ain't going to happen."

The boos became deafening. Hogan told the crowd that WCW had never informed him of this match before it was announced. He was refusing to wrestle Goldberg.

Then Hogan tried to take control of the situation.

"To show everybody here that I'm a fair man," said Hogan. "I'm bringing in an NWO brother. He's going to give Goldberg his first loss tonight."

"Just in case Goldberg gets real lucky," continued Hogan, "then, and only then, will I grace you with my presence and kill Goldberg 'Hollywood'-style right in the middle of the ring."

Hogan had set up yet another obstacle for Goldberg, whose track record had already proved that there were few obstacles that could stop him.

Hogan left the crowd with a closing comment directed at Goldberg, "I feel sorry when the other brother from the NWO embarrasses you out here tonight."

The "other brother" Hogan had selected was Scott Hall, another founding member of the NWO. Hall had held singles and tag team titles before, so he was definitely quality opposition for Goldberg. Hall certainly had the ability to hand Goldberg his first loss.

To Goldberg's credit, he didn't run to the executive committee to complain about Hogan's trickery. He dealt with it as he had dealt with everything else since he entered WCW: intensity and silence. He would do his talking in the ring.

Hall would have to be next. The match with Hogan would have to wait.

Hall's strategy was to frustrate Goldberg and force him to lose focus. When the bell rang, Hall gave Goldberg a shove as if to remind him not to overlook the man he was facing in the ring.

Goldberg did not need a reminder.

The two locked up. Goldberg shoved back.

Hall flew through the air and fell to the mat. He stood up and tried to shake off the effects of feeling Goldberg's power firsthand. As they locked up again, Hall thrust his shoulder into Goldberg's muscular chest, causing Goldberg to counter with a quick takedown. Hall was back on the mat.

The two exchanged holds and power moves. Goldberg was winning the strength contest, and he began to frustrate his opponent. Hall left the ring in an effort to break Goldberg's momentum.

It would take more than that to slow down Goldberg.

Having had enough of his stronger opponent, Hall summoned other NWO members to ringside with a simple wave of his hand. Their assistance was needed if he was to have any chance of keeping Goldberg away from Hogan and the World title.

But the NWO thugs were blocked by WCW wrestlers, and a ringside riot ensued. As Hall watched the melee outside the ring, Goldberg pulled him back into the ring. The only win Goldberg would accept was a clean pin.

Hall had other plans. He forced Goldberg's throat into the ropes and then clotheslined the U.S. champion. Hall saw the opportunity to finish off Goldberg and give him his first loss.

Suddenly, a burst of adrenaline shot through Goldberg as he flipped Hall through the air. A dizzy Hall staggered around the ring. As his opponent walked around dazed, Goldberg positioned himself for a spear. His shoulders violently connected with Hall's stomach.

The crowd went wild as Goldberg set up Hall for the jackhammer. Seconds later, Goldberg was 107–0—and had eliminated his last obstacle to the World title.

WCW U.S. heavyweight champion Bill Goldberg puts Scott Hall to the mat during their July 6, 1998, match in Atlanta.

Mike Tenay, a member of the WCW announcing team, enthusiastically exclaimed, "We have an answer to 'Who's next?' It's Hollywood Hogan for the World heavyweight title!"

Goldberg had a very short time to savor the victory. Indeed, Hogan was next.

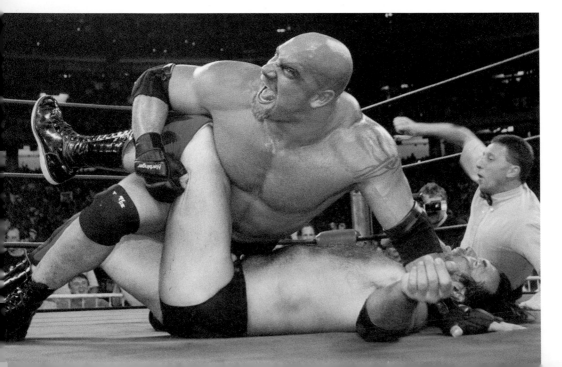

Within an hour, Goldberg's moment had arrived. He was standing in the ring with a wrestling legend, looking into the eyes of his destiny, eyes that belonged to WCW World champion Hogan.

Goldberg had to send a message to Hogan immediately. The two locked up and Goldberg immediately put Hogan in a headlock. A headlock is an elementary move in professional wrestling, but Goldberg's strength made the hold very punishing as he squeezed the champion's head.

An angry Hogan immediately started kicking, punching, and scratching Goldberg. Hogan pulled off his weight belt and started to whip the challenger. In pain, Goldberg grabbed the belt. He looked at the weapon and looked at Hogan. With disgust, Goldberg threw it out of the ring.

He already had an arsenal of weapons.

Goldberg's power was weakening the champion. So Hogan left the ring to gather his thoughts and recover his strength. And he chose a strategy. He wanted Goldberg out there with him.

Hogan returned to the ring, but not for long. He threw his opponent out and followed him. He forced Goldberg's head into the ringside barrier. Goldberg became groggy and started staggering. Hogan then took a chair and hit his opponent with it three times. The challenger was forced to his knees.

Had Goldberg finally met his match?

Sensing he had his opponent defeated, Hogan resumed his treachery back in the ring. He lifted Goldberg and bodyslammed him to the mat. His famous legdrop hit Goldberg three

38

Hollywood Hogan was reluctant to wrestle Goldberg and sent Scott Hall to stop the young challenger. One hour after Goldberg pinned Hall on July 6, 1998, Hogan had no choice but to step into the ring with Goldberg, who defeated him for the World title.

times. History has shown that very few men can recover from one Hogan legdrop, let alone three.

Suddenly the NWO's Curt Hennig came through the curtain. His motivation was unclear, as Hogan was not in danger of a title loss. In fact, at this point in the bout he was dominating Goldberg and hardly in need of any assistance. Hennig did not get a chance to help or harm Hogan. Karl Malone, a popular pro basketball player who was a WCW booster, attacked Hennig.

Hogan was distracted. He looked at Malone with disgust for attacking his NWO teammate, and, in doing so, failed to notice what was happening behind him in the ring.

Goldberg had recovered from the three Hogan legdrops.

As Hogan turned around, Goldberg speared him to the mat. Hollywood was paralyzed from the move. The crowd's cheers were deafening!

Goldberg looked at a television camera and signaled that history was about to be made.

Just as he had done to Scott Hall earlier in the night, Goldberg picked up Hogan and lifted him high in the air. The crash to the mat came seconds later. Another perfect jackhammer.

The referee counted. One, two, three.

A new World heavyweight champion was crowned.

The members of the audience jumped to their feet in celebration. Goldberg was handed both his U.S. belt and the World heavyweight title. Hogan rolled out of the ring in physical and emotional pain.

Goldberg was 108–0.

It was a moment not only of wrestling history, but of vindication for Goldberg. After injuries, disappointments, personal setbacks, and a strange new career direction, Goldberg had finally lived up to the high standards he had set for himself. All the advice and encouragement from family, friends, and coaches had led to this one moment: WCW World heavyweight champion Bill Goldberg.

5 THE SHOCKING LOSS

After winning the WCW World championship, Goldberg said "I never envisioned myself as a professional wrestler, let alone standing one-on-one against Hulk Hogan," In championship victory, Goldberg was gracious. To him, Hogan was more than just a ring villain; he was still a man who had made wrestling history. No matter how devious and evil Hogan's actions might have been, he remained, in Goldberg's eyes, a living legend. "Hulk Hogan has done more for the sport than a lot of people collectively," said Goldberg. "He's a legend. So, to wrestle him is one thing. To beat him is completely different."

In championship victory, Goldberg also discovered that winning the WCW World title was far easier than holding on to it.

"It's hard to describe the pressure that goes with being the World champion," Goldberg said in an interview. "Then again, no one can put more pressure on me than myself. Sure, it's a lot of pressure being World champion, but no more pressure than I put on myself."

One by one, the challengers lined up for their title shots. A match with Goldberg now had greater significance. Beating him was about more than just ending the longest unbeaten

---

One of WCW's most popular wrestlers, Goldberg, who is Jewish, says he hasn't heard many ethnic taunts or felt pressure from organizers to change his name.

rookie streak the sport had ever known. It was now about being top man in WCW.

"I'm in the arena every night and I don't, and won't, back down from anyone," said Goldberg "I'm a marked man as the World heavyweight champion, but I was a marked man before, too."

Members of the NWO, in particular, were demanding matches with the new champion. Eager to exact revenge on the man who had defeated their leader, they all wanted the opportunity to provide Goldberg with his first taste of defeat.

Curt Hennig would be the first NWO member to face Goldberg for the title. His effort came up short, though, as he became the next victim to succumb to the jackhammer. The Giant and Brian Adams, both tried, and The Giant and Brian Adams both failed. NWO Hollywood simply could not end the rule of Goldberg.

Even wrestlers loyal to WCW, like "Diamond" Dallas Page and Sting, wanted their chance to lead WCW as the World champion. Their efforts ultimately came up short, as they, too, fell victim to Goldberg's power and momentum.

Goldberg's unbeaten streak was growing to mythical proportions. Two other things were improving as well.

Goldberg's popularity was moving beyond just wrestling fans. He was being featured in articles for *Time*, *Newsweek*, and *USA Today*. Taking note of the fan reaction, news programs and talk shows requested appearances.

More important, his wrestling skills were improving as well.

In match after match, Goldberg was incorporating new moves to baffle his opponents.

Curt Hennig, the first NWO member to challenge Goldberg for the world title, failed, as did fellow NWO members Brian Adams and The Giant.

While wrestlers prepared to battle the champion by watching videotapes of his past matches, those matches didn't matter much. His style was constantly changing.

Goldberg incorporated a faster pace. He used martial arts moves and mat wrestling techniques. With every victory, Goldberg learned something new and improved himself for the next encounter. It seemed like he had a move to beat anyone and everyone.

While Goldberg was defending his title against Kevin Nash, Scott Hall (right) sneaked into the ring and attacked Goldberg with an electric cattle prod, delivering a high-voltage shock that sent the champion straight to the mat.

However, Goldberg hadn't faced everyone in WCW.

Kevin Nash was the leader of a splinter NWO group called the Wolfpac. He also had been one of the most popular men in WCW. His tag team partner, Scott Hall, had turned against him to stay with the original NWO. Nash's Wolfpac included men who had fought for WCW when the NWO was first formed. Konnan, Sting, Lex Luger, and Randy Savage wore the red and black Wolfpac colors with pride.

Nash's singles career was blooming. The transition from tag team wrestling to singles had been difficult for him, but he had overcome that obstacle. When the opportunity for a title match knocked, Nash did not hesitate to answer.

The knock came November 22, 1998, at World War III, WCW's annual pay-per-view event that features a 60-man, over-the-top-rope battle royal. To win the match and a shot at the WCW World title, a wrestler had to be the last man remaining in the ring. Nash's massive size, 7' and 356 pounds, was a tremendous advantage in this important bout. Experts picked him as an early favorite.

The experts were right. Nash easily won the battle royal and a shot at Goldberg.

Fans salivated at the prospect of a Nash-Goldberg bout. It would be Goldberg's jackknife versus Nash's jackknife powerbomb.

"I think Kevin Nash is one person who the fans would like to see me go up against. I ain't backing down, and I ain't afraid of anyone in this sport, or anyone in another sport, or anyone who walks the face of this earth, for that matter," said Goldberg. "There are a lot of people who think he will take control of me and give me my first loss, but I'm here to tell you that that ain't going to happen."

Speculation leading up to the December 27, 1998, match obviously focused on Goldberg's streak, which had grown to 173–0, and Nash's ability to end it.

For either of the two popular wrestlers, a victory could bestow legendary status. If Goldberg defeated Nash, he would continue his unprecedented streak by defeating his biggest challenger. If Nash defeated Goldberg, he would capture the World title and end a winning streak that had lasted for more than a year.

As the combatants entered the ring, the cheers of the fans were split about evenly. Both Nash and Goldberg played to the crowd, encouraging louder cheers for themselves. The energy from the fans fueled both men.

The opening bell rang, and brute strength met brute strength as the two locked up in the middle of the ring. Goldberg forced Nash into the ropes and pushed him. Goldberg wanted to remind Nash who was the champion and who was not. Nash needed no reminders.

Nash grabbed Goldberg and placed him in a headlock. As he forced his massive arm around the smooth head of the champion, Goldberg lifted Nash up with relative ease and slammed him backward into the mat.

The two men brawled, each one trying to get the better of the other. No one man could call himself the more dominant of the two. Suddenly, and without warning to anyone, let alone Nash, Goldberg drove his body into his opponent and speared him.

The fans rose to their feet. They sensed another Goldberg victory. A 174-match winning streak was at hand. Nash was about to be the latest answer to the frequently asked question: "Who's next?"

Goldberg held Nash by his long brown hair to position him for the jackknife. In doing so, Goldberg momentarily let his guard down. Nash capitalized on the opportunity. He struck Goldberg low, an illegal tactic borrowed from his rulebreaking days. Goldberg collapsed to the mat in pain.

With help from his friends, 7', 356-pound Kevin Nash was able to defeat Goldberg for the WCW World title on December 27, 1998, ending Goldberg's 173-match winning streak.

Seeing the advantage he had gained with one illegal move, Nash started to use more. His support from the fans continued in spite of his actions. They understood that in order to beat a man like Goldberg, an opponent couldn't hold anything back.

As Nash began to sense that victory was close, Goldberg stunned him again with a swinging neckbreaker, a move in which he wraps his beefy arms around his opponent's neck and throat and hurls him to the mat. Nash was stunned and lay flat on his back. Goldberg again signaled for the jackknife.

But chaos erupted as Disco Inferno, a rule-breaking wrestler who was trying to prove his merit for the Wolfpac, dashed to the ring. He was intent on helping Nash, but was met with a Goldberg assault that included a devastating spear.

Just as Disco Inferno was being removed from the ring, Bam Bam Bigelow, a newcomer to WCW at the time, ran to the ring. He had started a feud with Goldberg weeks earlier, and now saw an opportunity to sabotage Goldberg's title defense. Goldberg greeted him with a clothesline that forced him over the rope and onto the arena floor.

The referee tried to restore order in the match, but he did not succeed. Holding back Nash from going after Bigelow, the referee failed to notice what was going on behind him.

Scott Hall was becoming the third man to illegally enter the match, and on this occasion, the third time would be the charm for Kevin Nash's title hopes.

Hall possessed a weapon that Bigelow and Disco Inferno did not. He was carrying an electric cattle prod, a high-voltage shock stick, underneath his shirt. Hall forced the prod into Goldberg's chest, sending a blaze of electrical voltage through the champion's body. Goldberg collapsed to the mat, helpless and shaking.

Nash did not witness his former friend attack his opponent. Seeing Goldberg lying on the mat, Nash saw his chance to do what no other man could do in 173 matches before this amazing bout.

Nash picked up the semi-conscious champion and positioned his head between his legs, preparing for his signature move. He lifted Goldberg high in the air. He slammed his body into the mat.

Nash's jackknife powerbomb was devastating.

The referee counted Goldberg out as Nash covered him. Three seconds had changed wrestling history: Goldberg's reign as champion and the most famous unbeaten streak in wrestling history were over. The World champion was no longer world champion. Goldberg's 173–0 record had become a 173–1 record.

Goldberg had been defeated.

Now what?

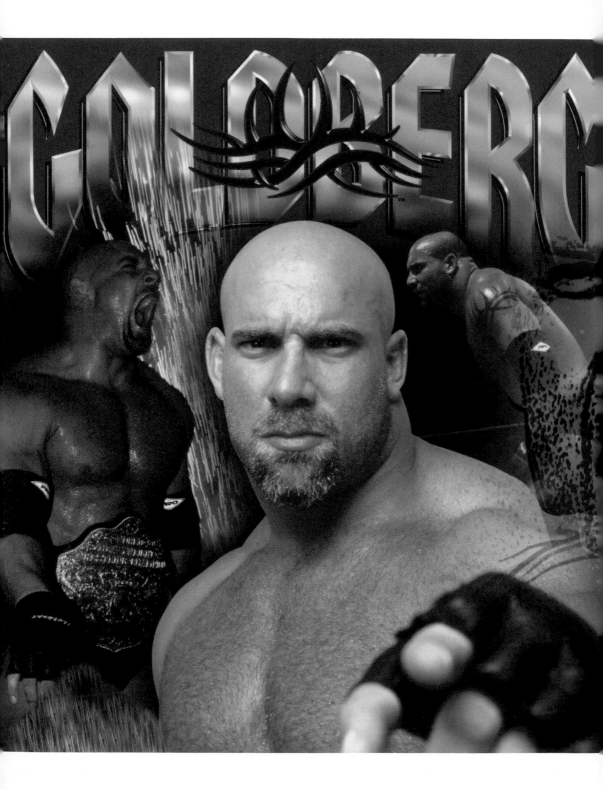

6 NEW CHALLENGES

One would think that the end of a monumental winning streak such as 173–0 would have plunged Goldberg into the depths of despair.

But Goldberg had known, ever since his days on the football field, that defeat was part of the game. For an athlete, defeat can result in one of two things: complaining, or using that defeat as a learning tool. Goldberg was not a complainer.

Although still a rookie, Goldberg understood that in wrestling, any man could beat any other man on any given night. So Goldberg, somewhere deep inside, probably saw defeat as inevitable.

But the circumstances surrounding his one loss were not acceptable to him.

If it was a clean pin in the middle of the ring, Goldberg would have chalked it up to a lack of experience in his young career. After all, Kevin Nash was a veteran who had many more years and many more matches behind him than his less-experienced foe.

Nash had not beaten him, though; a weapon had.

Still, the referee's decision was final, and Goldberg accepted the ruling without complaint.

Goldberg became WCW's leader in the war against the NWO, and he hoped this role would lead him back to the World title.

The fans who had followed Goldberg's streak did not hold back their support and devotion as a result of his loss. In fact, losing may have even increased Goldberg's popularity. The defeat made him more human, and therefore more of a figure to be admired.

The sportsmanlike way he handled this setback may have been the truest test of his character.

"There are a lot of people who want to see me fail, but that ain't going to happen because I have too much pride in myself, in what I do," said Goldberg. "Sure, I don't want to let down others, but, more than that, I don't want to let myself down."

Goldberg was back to the role of challenger and hunter, a role he knew very well from his background in football and his first year in wrestling.

After witnessing former partner Scott Hall's actions on video, the new World champion, Kevin Nash, was willing to grant Goldberg a rematch. He wanted to prove to the world that he could beat Goldberg without any outside assistance.

On the night of their rematch, Hollywood Hogan, who had announced his retirement weeks earlier on *The Tonight Show with Jay Leno*, returned to WCW. His appearance created plenty of suspicion. What were he and his NWO pals up to on this very important night?

Suddenly, without warning, Goldberg was arrested and taken away in handcuffs by the local police. The NWO's manager, Miss Elizabeth, had accused him of harassing her. Nash was angered, convinced that his old enemy, Hollywood Hogan was behind this situation. He demanded that if Goldberg could not make the match, then Hogan would take his place. WCW promoters agreed. Hogan was quick to accept the instant title opportunity.

Sadly, Goldberg's arrest and Nash's challenge to Hogan were all part of a fiendish plot that was revealed as soon as the "match" got underway.

The opening bell rang. The two men stood in the ring, and they appeared ready to wrestle. Then Hogan pointed his finger and poked it into Nash's massive chest. Nash fell to his back and lay motionless.

Fans were confused. How could one finger put down the World champion? But confusion became understanding all too quickly as Hogan covered Nash and the referee counted Nash down and declared Hollywood Hogan the World champion once again.

Then Nash stood up, and he and Hogan began to laugh and celebrate in the ring. Scott Hall joined in on the despicable scene. The NWO had emerged victorious, tricking the World title away from Goldberg and WCW.

After the police discovered Elizabeth had been lying, Goldberg was released from custody. He wasted little time in returning to the arena. Goldberg ran to the ring to gain a measure of revenge against the evil duo of Nash and Hogan. He had lost his opportunity for a rematch, but he was still ready for action. Goldberg was outraged at the scheme, not to mention the way in which Nash and Hogan had cheapened the World title.

Lex Luger was not far behind the former champion. But Luger was not helping Goldberg. To the astonishment of almost everyone on hand that night, Luger was helping the all-new NWO, of which he was the newest member, to attack Goldberg.

Goldberg was beaten, battered, and embarrassed by the NWO's group attack. But as with all other setbacks he had ever faced, he got up, brushed himself off, and prepared for the next challenge.

"Determination. I don't back away from confrontations, and it was that way also when I played football," said Goldberg. "When being attacked in the ring, I react, and go for a victory, or I'll die in the process!"

Goldberg's first goal is to get his winning ways back on track. He can't erase the one blemish on his perfect record, but that loss can't stop him from continuing his dominant and winning ways, or from taking on a new role.

With Sting recovering from an injury and Luger having defected to the NWO, Goldberg has become WCW's new leader in the renewed war with the New World Order. It is a responsibility that he welcomes.

It is a responsibility that he hopes will lead him back to the World title.

Goldberg's unlikely journey from football to professional wrestling has paid its dividends. He is thankful for the opportunities that have been presented to him, no matter what the outcome has been. No matter how many shock sticks knock him down, he will always get back up to fight a fair battle.

"It really takes my breath away to think where I was a year ago, and then to think where I'm at today," Goldberg says, reflecting on his short career. "I'm not going to mess with the success I've had. I'm very fortunate for the

success I've had, and hopefully I can do something positive with it."

Goldberg takes his status as a role model seriously. Because he is an animal lover, Goldberg serves as a spokesman for the Humane Society of the United States (HSUS), an organization working to prevent animal cruelty. Goldberg has done public service announcements for the HSUS in which he says "Animal fighting is not a sport; it's a crime!" His picture also appears on HSUS posters and other promotional materials.

At a Congressional briefing in February of 1999 Goldberg announced his support for federal legislation that would help eliminate cockfighting, which is the practice of pitting roosters against one another in a fight to the death. Cockfighting is legal only in Louisiana,

Humane Society spokesman Bill Goldberg signs autographs for fans after speaking out against cruelty to animals. Goldberg supprts legislation that would eliminate cockfighting, which is currently legal in three states, including his home state of Oklahoma.

Goldberg's critics accused him of copying "Stone Cold" Steve Austin (right) who also favors plain black trunks and a cold demeanor. But Goldberg insists that he is his own man and has challenged Austin to a match "any time, any place."

New Mexico, and Oklahoma. However, it continues to take place illegally in many areas of the country, and spectators frequently place bets on the outcomes of the fights.

In his opposition to cockfighting, Goldberg has made a clear distinction between humans who choose to fight one another for sport and animals who are forced to fight. "Cockfighters pump roosters full of stimulants, affix steel blades to their legs, and force them to fight to the death," Goldberg said at a press conference for the HSUS. "When I fight, I choose to step into the ring, but animals are forced to fight and suffer and die in the process."

Goldberg has personally visited many members of Congress, urging them to pass legislation that would end the cruel treatment of animals. He has also vowed to end cockfighting in his home state of Oklahoma, and is working with organizers to help pass a citizen ballot initiative that would make cockfighting illegal.

Goldberg hungers for challenges. He is always looking for new mountains to climb. He is always seeking out opportunities to become a better wrestler. He longs for new opponents to add to his list of victims. Beating the same wrestler night after night does little to advance Goldberg's skills.

A wrestler doesn't even have to wrestle in WCW to catch Goldberg's attention. He is an equal-opportunity predator.

His next challenge: WWF superstar "Stone Cold" Steve Austin.

The intense competition between WCW and the WWF does not allow the two to promote any events together. Typically, the wrestlers from each organization pay little attention to each other.

If Goldberg has taught his fans anything, though, that lesson would be that he is anything but typical.

When *The Tonight Show* invited Goldberg to make an appearance on February 19, 1999, he agreed. During his interview by host Jay Leno, Goldberg was asked about his feelings towards Austin. The former WCW World champion smirked and wasted little time in issuing the challenge to Stone Cold. Goldberg focused his eyes on the camera and directed his words at Austin.

"Ever since I started, everyone always called me a rip-off of Steve Austin," Goldberg said in a menacing tone. "And I don't know what he's thinking, or if he's even thinking. I'll throw a hundred grand of my money, Austin. Any time, any place. We can even do it in the back alley of the NBC studios."

The crowd cheered wildly. Leno was shocked. WCW, while not in the habit of mentioning wrestlers from other organizations, stood behind their former champ. If Goldberg wanted Austin, who was going to stop him?

Goldberg had not only acknowledged a wrestler from another promotion, but he had dared Austin to respond to his offer. While their look may be the same—bald head, black tights, menacing presence—Goldberg wanted to prove who was the better man. He wanted to prove that he was an innovator, not an imitator.

The prospect of such a dream match, while unrealistic, is exciting. Goldberg's words appeared in newspapers and magazines around the world the day after the broadcast, but Austin and the WWF chose to ignore the challenge. WCW has yet to press the issue. However, Goldberg's offer stands, no matter when, no matter where.

It is just another dream to realize for the man who has realized so many other dreams.

If Goldberg's rookie year in wrestling is any indication of his future career, wrestlers will continue to feel plenty of spears and jackhammers.

Goldberg continues to set higher standards for himself, and as a result he continues to take the sport to greater heights. Because when Goldberg reaches a goal, he has made it clear that he will create another one even more difficult to achieve. And as he achieves his goals, he is always aware of the image that he is sending out to the children who watch him on television. He takes his status as a role model very seriously. The lessons he learned from his parents about fair play and respect remain with him.

"It's a big responsibility to take on, but I take on that responsibility with open arms," he said. "I'd say, 'Be proud of what you are and who you are, and you can do anything you set your mind to.'"

Goldberg is a living example of his own straightforward advice.

The first year of his career was amazing . . . and the years to come should be at least as incredible.

We're fortunate to be living in the Goldberg era of pro wrestling.

Chronology

1966   Born in Tulsa, Oklahoma, on December 27.

1990   Drafted by the Los Angeles Rams

1992–94   Plays pro football with the Atlanta Falcons.

1995   Drafted by the Carolina Panthers football team.

1996   Signs a contract with WCW.

1997   Makes WCW wrestling debut and defeats Hugh Morrus.

Debuts on pay-per-view at Starrcade and pins Steve McMichael.

1998   Defeats Raven at *Monday Nitro* for the WCW U.S. heavyweight title.

Defeats Sting in Pittsburgh, Pennsylvania.

Defeats Hollywood Hogan at *Monday Nitro* for the WCW World heavyweight title.

Defeats Curt Hennig at Bash at the Beach in his first title defense.

Pins "Diamond" Dallas Page at Halloween Havoc.

Loses WCW World title to Kevin Nash.

1999   Becomes spokesman for the Humane Society of the United States.

Further Reading

Burkett, Harry. "Goldberg: A Giant Step Away from Immortality."
   The Wrestler (September 1998): 56–59.

Burkett, Harry. "Goldberg Without the Gold: 'Now My Career
   Really Begins.'" *Wrestling Superstars* (June 1999): 14–17.

Burnett, Larry. "Goldberg! The Ironic Inside Story." *WOW Magazine*
   (May 1999): 12–31.

Ethier, Bryan. "For Goldberg, the Wrestling Ring Was His
   True Field of Dreams." *Wrestler Extra: True Life Stories* 2
   (Winter 1998): 76–86.

Rosenbaum, Dave. "The Goldberg Streak: It's Your Fault It's Over."
   Inside Wrestling (May 1999): 34-37.

Index

Adams, Brian, 42
Anderson, Arn, 21
Andre the Giant, 30
Austin, Steve, 10, 57, 58
Barbarian, the, 23, 24
Bigelow, Bam Bam 48
Bruce, Dwayne, 21
Cherry, Jim, 16
Dillon, James J., 33
Disco Inferno, 48
Dooley, Vince, 17, 18
Edison High School,
    15, 16
Elizabeth, Miss, 52, 53
Georgia Bulldogs, 17
Giant, The, 30, 42.
    See also Paul Wight
Glacier, 25
Goldberg, Bill
    as Atlanta Falcon, 19
    birth, 15
    as Carolina Panther, 20
    childhood, 15–17
    and Humane Society
        of the United States,
        55–57
    injured, 19–20
    as Los Angeles Ram, 18

pro wrestling debut
    with WCW, 7
with Sacramento Surge, 19
WCW U.S. title, 29
WCW World title, 39
Goldberg, Ethel, 15, 24
Goldberg, Jed, 15
Goldberg, Mike, 15
Goldberg, Steve, 15
Hall, Scott, 34–36, 39, 44,
    48, 52, 53
Hennig, Curt, 38, 42,
Hogan, Hulk, 28, 31, 33–39,
    41, 52, 53
Humane Society of the
    United States, 55, 57
Konnan, 44
Leno, Jay, 57, 58
Luger, Lex, 19, 21, 44,
    53, 54
Malone, Karl, 38, 39
McMichael, Steve, 26
Monday Nitro, 7, 8, 29,
    33, 34
Morris, Hugh, 8–12, 23, 24
Nash, Kevin, 44–49, 51–53
National Football League
    (NFL), 18, 19

New World Order (NWO),
    27, 34, 35, 38, 39, 42,
    44, 52–54
Page, Dallas, 19, 29, 42
Power Plant, the, 9, 21
Raven, 29
Ray, Stevie, 25
Riggs, Scotty, 25
Savage, Randy, 44
Sting, 19, 21, 30, 42, 44,
    54
Tenay, Mike, 36
Tonight Show, The, 52, 57
Tulsa, Oklahoma, 15, 17
University of Georgia, 17
University of Minnesota, 15
Wight, Paul, 30
Wolfpac, the, 44, 48
World Championship
    Wrestling (WCW), 7–9, 19,
    21, 23, 26–31, 33–39,
    41–42, 44, 45, 48, 52–54,
    57, 58
World Football League, 19
World Wrestling Federation
    (WWF), 10, 30, 57, 58
Wrath, 25

Photo Credits

All-Star Sports: p. 22; Associated Press/Wide World Photos: p. 36; Courtesy Atlanta
Falcons: pp. 10, 14; Courtesy Georgia Bulldogs: p. 20; University of Minnesota Sports
Information: p. 17; Humane Society of the United States/Hilary Schwab: p. 55;
Jeff Eisenberg Sports Photography: pp. 25, 43, 44, 47; Sports Action: pp. 40, 56, 60;
WCW: pp. 2, 6, 28, 32, 38, 50.

KYLE ALEXANDER has been involved in the publication of professional wrestling magazines for a decade, both as a writer and an illustrator. His work has been featured prominently in professional wrestling publications all over the world. During the past 10 years, he has made numerous appearances on radio and television, offering his unique perspective on the "sport of kings."